How I Use AI (and When I Don't)

A Human-Centered Guide to Thinking With AI

Monique DuPree

LIVING LIBRARY PRESS

This book is intended for informational and educational purposes only. The author makes no representations or warranties regarding the accuracy or completeness of the information contained herein.

The content of this book does not constitute legal, medical, financial, technological, or professional advice. Readers are responsible for exercising their own judgment and seeking appropriate professional guidance where necessary.

Artificial intelligence tools and technologies referenced in this book may change over time. The author does not guarantee ongoing functionality, accuracy, or availability of any specific system or platform.

Published by Living Library Press

First Edition

ISBN: (Paperback ISBN here)
ISBN: (eBook ISBN here)

Published by Living Library Press
Davenport, Florida

This Book Is

This book is a reflection on how I use artificial intelligence thoughtfully, intentionally, and within boundaries.

It is a guide to thinking *with* AI — not outsourcing thinking to it.

It is human-centered.

It is calm.

It is practical and steady.

It does not require technical expertise.

It is written for people who want clarity, not speed.

It is for thinkers, creators, professionals, and everyday individuals who want to remain grounded while using powerful tools.

It is about posture before productivity.

It is about judgment before automation.

It is about remembering that tools serve people — not the other way around.

This Book Is Not

This book is not a prompt encyclopedia.

It is not a technical manual.

It is not a productivity hack guide.

It is not an attempt to replace discernment with software.

It is not an endorsement of blind trust in any system.

It does not promote automation over wisdom.

It does not assume AI is neutral or infallible.

It does not claim to have all the answers.

It simply models a way of engaging with AI that preserves human responsibility, clarity, and restraint.

Dedication

For my children and the generations after them —

May you use every tool available to you
without ever surrendering your mind, your judgment,
or your humanity.

Content

Part I

Posture Before Use

Chapter 1

The Tool Is Not the Thinker

The first thing I had to understand about artificial intelligence was simple:
It is a tool.

It is not a mind.
It is not a conscience.
It is not a voice of authority.
It is not a replacement for human judgment.

It responds.
That's all.

AI systems do not think the way humans think.
They do not reason independently, form beliefs, or possess wisdom.

They generate responses based on patterns.
They analyze input and predict likely output.
They rearrange information.
But they do not own it.

That distinction matters more than anything else in this book.

The moment we confuse a tool with a thinker, we begin surrendering responsibility.
The responsibility belongs to us.

Why This Matters

Many people are either overly impressed by AI or deeply afraid of it.
Both reactions come from the same misunderstanding.
We mistake fluency for intelligence.

If something responds quickly and confidently, we assume it must understand.
But speed is not understanding.
Fluency is not wisdom.
And output is not ownership.

AI can produce paragraphs in seconds.
It does not care whether they are true.
It does not weigh moral consequences.
It does not consider long-term impact.
It does not feel the cost of being wrong.

Humans do.

That is the right order.
The tool serves the thinker.
Not the other way around.

When I first started using AI, I didn't understand what it was. I assumed it was something like a faster version of Google — a search engine with better phrasing. I didn't realize that how I used it mattered. I didn't realize that the quality of my thinking would shape the quality of its responses. And I certainly didn't realize that if I approached it without boundaries, I could slowly outsource my own judgment without noticing.

That realization changed everything.

The difference between using a tool and leaning on it is subtle at first. It doesn't feel like surrender. It feels efficient. It feels helpful. It feels productive.

Thinking is a muscle.
Muscles weaken when they are not used.

AI can assist your thinking.

It should never replace it.
Understanding that AI is a tool is not limiting. It is freeing.

When you understand the order, you understand your role.
And when you understand your role, you can use powerful tools without being shaped by them.

The goal is not to avoid technology.
The goal is to remain responsible for how you use it.

In the next chapter, we'll talk about the boundaries that make that possible.

Chapter 2

Why Boundaries Come First

The more capable AI becomes, the more important it is to decide how and when you will use it.
Power without limits rarely ends well.

AI can generate ideas in seconds.
It can draft emails.
It can organize research.
It can summarize pages of information almost instantly.

But capability is not the same thing as control.
Boundaries determine control.

If you do not decide how you will use AI, you will slowly begin reacting to what it gives you instead of directing it.
That shift is subtle.
It happens quickly.

What Boundaries Actually Look Like

A boundary is not fear.
It is clarity.

It is deciding ahead of time:

- What you will use AI for
- What you will not use it for
- Where you will verify information
- Where final decisions belong

When you decide ahead of time how you will use a tool, you are less likely to let it decide for you in the moment.
That is the difference between assistance and dependence.

A Simple Example

Let's say someone types:
Who's hiring near me?"

That sounds reasonable.
It is still unclear.

What kind of job?
What pay range?
What schedule?
What commute distance?
What long-term goal?

Without boundaries, the tool fills in the blanks.
When someone is anxious or overwhelmed, they may accept whatever sounds confident.

Confidence in a response is not the same thing as ownership of a decision.
Ownership always belongs to the person who acts.

The Boundary Version

Now compare that with this:

"Based on my resume, help me identify roles that match my experience in customer service and operations.
Limit results to positions within a 20-minute commute.
Exclude commission-only roles.
Highlight opportunities with growth potential."

Notice what changed.
The tool did not choose a future.

The person defined their limits first.

They set:

- Skill alignment
- Commute boundary
- Compensation preference
- Advancement value

The tool now filters.
It does not decide.

What AI Might Return

Operations Coordinator – 12 minutes away – $55–65K – clear advancement path
Customer Experience Supervisor – 18 minutes away – salary + benefits
Logistics Support Manager – 15 minutes away – growth track into regional leadership

Clean. Organized. Within constraints.

The clarity of the output reflects the clarity of the request.
AI rewards specificity.
It does not assume responsibility.

The Hidden Risk

The risk is not that AI will take control.
The risk is that we will slowly hand it over.

If we ask vaguely, we receive vaguely.
If we ask lazily, we receive broadly.
If we do not define our limits, we adapt to what sounds persuasive.

That is how subtle dependence begins.
Not with one dramatic decision.
But with repeated unexamined ones

The Principle

Boundaries must come before capability.
Because once a tool becomes powerful, it becomes easy to lean on it.

When you lean too far, you stop trusting your own judgment.

Thinking is a muscle.
Muscles weaken when they are not used.

In the next chapter, we'll talk about something most people chase when they use AI:
Speed.

Speed without clarity creates confusion.
Clarity must come first.

Chapter 3

Clarity Before Speed

AI is fast.
That is what most people notice first.

It answers instantly.
It generates quickly.
It produces in seconds what used to take hours.

Speed is impressive.
Speed is addictive.
But speed is not the same thing as wisdom.
Speed without clarity creates confusion.

What Clarity Actually Means

Clarity is not complicated.

Clarity means you know what you want and what you don't.
Clarity means you have decided your intention before you ask.
Clarity means you are not outsourcing your thinking — you are organizing it.

When clarity comes first, speed becomes helpful.
When speed comes first, clarity disappears.
That is when frustration begins.

Why Speed Feels So Good

Speed feels powerful.
It feels efficient.
It feels modern.
It feels like progress.

But if you ask a vague question quickly,
you will receive a vague answer quickly.

The problem is not the speed.
The problem is the lack of direction.

AI does not slow you down.
It amplifies what you give it.

If you are scattered, it will organize scattered input.
If you are clear, it will organize clarity.

The output reflects the clarity of the request.

The Cultural Obsession

We live in a culture that rewards speed.
Fast responses.
Fast production.
Fast decisions.

AI fits perfectly into that rhythm.

Here is the quiet disruption:

You do not have to move as fast as the tool.
You can pause.
You can think.
You can refine the question before you press enter.

That pause is not weakness.
It is leadership.

A Better Way to Use Speed

Instead of asking quickly, ask clearly.

Instead of saying:
Help me fix this."

Try:
Help me refine this message to be calm, direct, and professional.
Keep it under 200 words.
Remove emotional language."

Now speed becomes precision.
Not noise.

The Real Shift

When you prioritize clarity:
You ask better questions.
You set better boundaries.
You make better decisions.

AI is powerful.
But it does not replace your judgment.
It accelerates your judgment.

That is why clarity must come first.
Speed is not the goal.

Sound thinking is.
Sound thinking is slower than typing.

AI can move quickly.
You do not have to.

The tool is not the thinker.
You are.

Chapter 4

Assistance, Not Dependence

AI is a tool designed to assist.
That word matters.
Assist.

It means support.
It means reinforcement.
It means help.
It does not mean replace.

There is a difference between assistance and dependence.
That difference is subtle at first.

Assistance strengthens your thinking.
Dependence quietly reduces your involvement.

The shift rarely feels dramatic.
It feels efficient.

You begin by asking for help organizing your thoughts.
Then you begin asking it to draft before you've thought it through.

Then you begin reacting to what it gives you instead of forming your own position first.

Nothing feels wrong.
Something has changed.

You are no longer leading the process.
You are responding to it.

That is what I call flow drift.
It does not happen in one decision.
It happens in small, nearly invisible adjustments.

The moment assistance becomes automatic instead of intentional, your engagement begins to shrink.
Because the output is fast and polished, the loss is easy to miss.

So how do you prevent that?

You stay active.

Before you open AI, pause.

Ask yourself:
What do I already think?
What do I already know?
What am I trying to say?

Even a single sentence written in your own words keeps you anchored in the process.

Then you invite AI to assist.
To refine.
To organize.
To expand.
To challenge.
Not to replace.

Here is the principle:

AI helps.
It should not take over.

Used with intention, you stay in charge.
That is the line.

Assistance protects your ability to think.
Dependence slowly weakens it.

Weakness rarely announces itself.
It just feels easier.
Easier is not always better.

PART II

THINKING WITH AI

Chapter 5

Asking Better Questions

Speed is impressive.

AI responds quickly. It does not respond intelligently on its own.

It responds to what you give it.

If your request is vague, the output will be vague.
If your request is shallow, the output will feel generic.
If your request is thoughtful and specific, the output becomes sharper.

AI rewards clarity.

The quality of the answer reflects the quality of the question.

That is not a limitation.
It is a mirror.

Most people ask broad questions and then blame the tool for broad answers.

"Find me a job."

That sounds reasonable.
But it is incomplete.

Compare that to:

"Find customer service positions within 25 miles of my home that are hiring for morning shifts and pay at least $18 an hour."

The second question creates direction.
It sets boundaries.
It narrows the focus.

Now you are not just asking for help.

You are guiding the tool.
When you guide it well, the output improves.

You can go further.

Instead of saying:

"Help me improve my resume."

Try:

"Based on this resume, identify roles within 25 miles of my location that match my experience. Then suggest adjustments I can make to better match my resume to those positions."

That is not complexity.

That is intention.

Better questions produce better structure.
Better structure produces better thinking.

AI does not think for you.
It will follow the direction you provide.

If you rush the question, you rush the outcome.
If you clarify the question, you clarify the result.

The shift is small.
It changes everything.

In the next chapter, we'll explore what happens after the answer arrives — and how to use structure without surrendering ownership.

Chapter 6

Organizing Thought Without Losing Ownership

You do not lose ownership the moment you use AI.
You lose ownership when you stop thinking.

There is a difference.

AI is exceptionally good at structure.
It can:

Reorder your ideas
Group themes
Tighten language
Summarize concepts
Outline complex thoughts
Highlight patterns you missed

That is assistance.
But assistance only works properly when the ideas are yours.

If you give AI a developed thought and ask it to organize, it sharpens your work.
If you give AI a blank space and ask it to create your thinking, it replaces your work.

That distinction matters.

What Organization Actually Looks Like

Let's say you have written a messy page of ideas about a project.

Instead of asking:
Create a full plan for me."

You ask:
Here are my ideas. Can you organize them into clear categories and suggest a logical order?"

That is structure.
Not surrender.

Or maybe you have drafted a paragraph and it feels scattered.

Instead of asking:
Rewrite this."

You ask:
Can you help me make this clearer while keeping my main point intact?"

The thinking is still yours.
AI is refining it.
Ownership stays with you because the ideas began with you.

The Subtle Risk

The risk is not organization.
The risk is skipping the thinking phase entirely.

If you never struggle through your own thoughts,
you never strengthen your judgment.

If you never draft your own ideas,
you never discover your own voice.

AI can clean up your thinking.
It cannot build your foundation.
If it does, that foundation will be fragile.

A Simple Check

Before asking AI to organize something, pause and ask yourself:

Can I explain this idea out loud without assistance?

If the answer is yes,
you are organizing.
If the answer is no,
you may be outsourcing.

That pause keeps you in control of your own thinking.

Why This Matters

Structure feels powerful.
Clean outlines feel impressive.
Polished summaries feel intelligent.
But polish without ownership is fragile.

If someone asks you to explain your idea,
you should not need AI to defend it for you.

You should understand it.
You should believe it.
You should be able to stand behind it.

AI can help you clarify.
It should never replace your conviction.

The Balance

Use AI to:

Structure
Refine
Condense
Expand thoughtfully
Test flow

Do not use AI to:

Decide what you believe
Determine your position
Replace your effort
Form opinions you have not considered yourself

Organization is support.
Ownership is responsibility.
Keep both.

In the next chapter, we move even deeper.
We will look at how to use AI to generate ideas without confusing suggestion with truth.

Ideas are powerful.
Not every idea deserves adoption.

Chapter 7

When AI Helps Me Think Clearly

AI does not think for me.
It can help me think more clearly.

There is a difference.

Clarity is not speed.
Clarity is not polish.
Clarity is seeing your own thoughts without distortion.

Sometimes our thinking is crowded.

Too many ideas.
Too many emotions.
Too many angles at once.
That mental clutter is normal.
AI can help reduce the noise.

What Clear Thinking Actually Looks Like

Sometimes I already know what I believe.

I just can't articulate it.

I may have a conviction,
a concern,
or a perspective,
but it feels tangled.

When I describe it honestly,
AI can reflect it back in a structured way.

Not new thinking.
Clearer thinking.

It may say:
 It sounds like your main concern is…"

Suddenly I can see my own thought more plainly.

That's not outsourcing.
That's refinement.

Reflection, Not Replacement

AI works best as a mirror.

You bring the content.
It helps you organize what you already carry.

When I explain something in detail,
AI may highlight themes,
summarize patterns,
or clarify contradictions.

It only works with what I give it.
If I give it confusion,
it helps untangle.
If I give it clarity,

it sharpens.

It does not create conviction.
It reveals structure.

The Discipline Required

There is responsibility here.

If I ask:
 Tell me what to think about this."
I surrender my position.

If I ask:
 Help me examine my reasoning."
I strengthen my position.

That difference matters.

Clear thinking requires ownership.
AI can assist.
It cannot decide.

Why This Is Powerful

When used correctly, AI becomes:

A sounding board
A clarity tool
A pattern identifier
A structured mirror

It can help you see gaps.
It can help you test assumptions.
It can help you refine language.

The thinking remains yours.
That is the point.

A Simple Practice

If you feel overwhelmed by a thought, try this:

Write exactly what you believe—even if it's messy.

Then ask:
Can you organize this and tell me what the core issue seems to be?"

Read the answer slowly.

Not to accept it blindly.
To evaluate it.

Does it reflect what you meant?
If yes, clarity increased.
If no, refine your explanation.

That process strengthens your thinking.

Clear thinking is not automatic.
It requires effort.
AI does not remove that effort.
It can help you channel it.

When used with discipline,
AI becomes less about answers
and more about understanding.

Understanding lasts longer.

In the next chapter, we'll explore something even more important:
how to test what AI gives you
without confusing coherence with truth.

Clear language
is not the same as correct information.

Chapter 8

When I Stop

Speed is powerful.
Clarity is grounding.
Structure is helpful.
But none of it replaces this:
The ability to stop.

There is a moment in every interaction with AI when you have enough.

Enough information.
Enough suggestions.
Enough refinement.
Continuing would not make it clearer.
It would only make it louder.

That is when you stop.

AI can keep going.
It can suggest another angle.
Another version.
Another variation.

Another improvement.
It does not tire.
It does not hesitate.
But you must.

Not because the tool is wrong.
Because thinking requires space.

Space cannot exist if you never pause.

When I stop, I am not rejecting assistance.
I am reclaiming reflection.

There is a difference.

Stopping says:
I have what I need for now."
"I will sit with this."
"I will decide."

Without stopping, the process becomes endless refinement.
Endless tweaking.
Endless asking.
Endless optimizing.

Somewhere inside all of that activity,
your own voice becomes faint.

Not erased.
Just quieter.

Over time, quieter becomes harder to hear.

The discipline of stopping is simple:
When the answer arrives, ask yourself:
Have I thought about this on my own yet?

If the answer is yes, continue carefully.
If the answer is no, pause.

Close the window.
Walk away.
Let your mind move without assistance.

This is not about distrust.
It is about maturity.

Tools are most powerful
when they are not constantly in your hand.
Strength is not in continuous use.
Strength is in knowing when use is complete.

When I stop, I remind myself:
I am thinking with AI.
Not through it.
Not instead of myself.
With it.

When I stop,
I prove that I can still think without it.

That is the difference.
That is the boundary.
That is the balance.
Part II ends here.

Before we move forward,
you must know this:

You can walk away.
And if you can walk away,
you are still in control.

Part III

Where I Draw the Line

Chapter 9

The Mirror Effect

AI does not create your thinking.
It reflects it.

That is the part most people miss.

When you type a question, the system does not reach inside you and replace your mind.
It works with what you provide.

The tone of your request, the depth of your thinking, the clarity of your instruction — all of it shapes what comes back.

If you ask vaguely, you receive something vague.
If you ask with structure, you receive something structured.
If you rush, the response will feel rushed.

The output mirrors the input.

That is not magic.

It is mechanics.

The effect feels personal.

When you begin using AI intentionally, you start noticing something:
the quality of the response improves when your thinking improves.

That realization can be uncomfortable.

It means the tool is not the limitation.
Your clarity might be.

That is not criticism.
It is opportunity.

When you refine your question, the answer sharpens.
When you provide context, the response gains depth.
hen you slow down and think first, the tool works better.

The mirror reveals your patterns.

Are you precise or scattered?

Curious or reactive?
Clear or rushing?
AI will not judge you.
It will simply respond.
And in that response, you will often see yourself.

That is the mirror effect.

Used casually, it is just convenience.
Used intentionally, it becomes feedback.

Not feedback about the machine.
Feedback about you.

That is where growth begins.

Once you realize the quality of your input shapes the quality of your output, you stop blaming the tool.

You start improving your thinking.
You begin asking better questions.
You slow down before typing.
You organize before requesting.
You clarify before expecting clarity in return.

That shift is subtle.
But it changes everything.

The mirror is not there to flatter you.
It is there to show you.
And when you are willing to look, you improve.

Not because AI made you smarter.
Because you chose to be more intentional.

That is the real power.

Chapter 10

Verification, Ownership, and Responsibility

AI can summarize faster than you can read.
It can condense pages into paragraphs, arguments into bullet points, and complexity into something that feels clean and manageable.

That's powerful.
But power always requires stewardship.

Here's where the shift happens.

You ask:
Summarize this article for me."

It responds instantly — clear, confident, structured.
The language sounds polished.
The points feel complete.
It even reads like something you could confidently repeat.

So you skim it.
It seems accurate.
You copy it.
You paste it.
You send it.

Your name is now attached to it.
But you never read the original article.

You didn't verify the source.
You didn't check whether anything important was omitted.
You didn't notice if nuance was flattened or if context was missing.

Nothing malicious happened.
Nothing dramatic.
Just speed replacing verification.

This is where leadership quietly separates itself from convenience.

Verification means you are willing to check.
Ownership means you are willing to stand behind what you share.
Responsibility means your name carries weight — not just speed.

AI can help you organize information, surface patterns, and summarize material quickly.
It can reduce friction.
It can save time.
It can even help you understand complex ideas more efficiently.
But it cannot carry your integrity for you.

If your name is on it, your responsibility is on it.

And this isn't only about AI.
It's about habits.

Forwarding headlines you didn't read.
Repeating claims you didn't examine.
Quoting summaries you didn't verify.

AI does not create those habits.
It reveals them.

Here's the quiet standard:

Read before you repeat.
Verify before you forward.
Clarify before you claim.

Not because you're afraid.
Because you lead.

The real question isn't,
 Can AI summarize this for me?"

It's this:

"Am I willing to own what I'm about to share?"

That's verification.
That's ownership.
That's responsibility.

And that's what separates users from leaders.

Chapter 11

Knowing When to Stop

AI can keep going.
It will generate more ideas.
More variations.
More summaries.
More angles.

You can refine forever.

That's the temptation.

But clarity does not always come from more input.
Sometimes it comes from silence.

There is a moment when the answer is sufficient.

There is a moment when refining becomes over-refining.

There is a moment when you stop thinking with the tool and return to thinking on your own.

This is not rejection.

It is rhythm.

You use the tool.
Then you step back.

You review.
You sit with what was generated.
You decide what stays and what goes.

And sometimes, you close it completely.

Because thinking is not outsourcing.
It is partnership.

Healthy use includes ending.

If you find yourself asking for five more versions,
three more angles,
two more rewrites —

Pause.

Ask yourself:

Am I refining…
or avoiding deciding?

That question changes everything.

AI can extend the process indefinitely.

But leadership includes conclusion.

There is power in saying:

"This is enough."

There is strength in making the final call.

There is maturity in knowing when the tool has served its purpose
and when it is time to move forward without it.

The goal is not constant optimization.

The goal is clear thinking.

And clear thinking does not require endless output.

Sometimes it requires restraint.

Close the tab.
Make the decision.
Move.

That is not limitation.

That is ownership.

Chapter 12

The Line I Will Not Cross

AI can help you think faster.
It can help you organize ideas.
It can help you explore angles you might not have considered.

But it can also help you bypass effort.

It can help you say things you did not fully understand.
It can help you sound informed without being informed.
It can help you move quickly past responsibility.

That is where the line appears.

Not a technical line.
A personal one.

Every tool has a boundary.
The boundary is not coded into the system.
It is coded into the person using it.

Before you use AI, decide:

What will I never ask this tool to do for me?

Will you let it replace your learning?
Will you let it replace your discernment?
Will you let it replace your accountability?

Or will you use it to strengthen those things?

There is a difference between assistance and avoidance.
Between support and substitution.
Between thinking with a tool
and letting the tool think instead of you.

Your line might be different than someone else's.
But you need one.

The most dangerous moment is not misuse.
It is unconscious drift.

When you slowly begin relying on it for decisions you should still be making.
When convenience starts feeling like capability.
When speed starts feeling like wisdom.

That is where you stop.

Not because the tool is bad.
Because you are responsible.

You decide:
This helps me organize.
This helps me explore.
This helps me clarify.

But this does not decide for me.
This does not replace my growth.

This does not carry my integrity.
That is the line.

Not dramatic.
Not fearful.
Not defensive.
Clear.

The strongest AI users are not the ones who use it the most.
They are the ones who know exactly where their boundary is.
And they do not cross it.

Chapter 13

Everyday Ways to Use AI Thoughtfully

AI does not have to be dramatic to be powerful.

It does not have to write speeches,
design business strategies,
or produce complex analysis.

Sometimes its most responsible use
is the most ordinary.

You can use it to:

Clarify a confusing email before you send it.
Summarize meeting notes so you can think clearly about next steps.
Organize scattered ideas into a cleaner outline.
Break down a complicated concept into plain language.

That is thoughtful use.
Not replacing your voice.

Refining it.

You can ask it:

"Help me make this clearer."
"Is there anything I'm missing?"
"Organize this so I can see it better."
"Explain this in simpler terms."

Notice the posture.

You are not asking it to decide.
You are asking it to assist.

It becomes a second pair of eyes.
A structural editor.
A thinking companion.
And sometimes, that's enough.

It can also help you improve how you work
without taking over your work.

You might ask it to:

Review a draft and suggest clearer wording.
Help you structure a proposal before you present it.
Identify gaps in your reasoning before someone else does.
Offer alternative approaches you hadn't considered.

That doesn't replace your job.
It strengthens your preparation.
It sharpens your thinking.
It helps you show up more organized, more thoughtful, more precise.

The value is not in handing over your responsibility.
The value is in refining how you carry it.
You can also use it to:

Compare options before making a purchase.
Draft a rough outline before writing a paper.
Generate questions you hadn't considered.
Translate technical language into something accessible.

But every time, the same standard applies:

You review.
You adjust.
You decide.

The tool supports clarity.
You maintain ownership.

Thoughtful use is not about doing more.
It is about thinking better.

Thinking better often looks ordinary.

It looks like slowing down before responding.
Like checking your understanding before sharing.
Like asking for structure before reacting.

AI can accelerate thought.
But thoughtful use stabilizes it.

That is the difference.

Chapter 14

Prompts That Encourage Thinking (Not Replacing It)

Not all prompts are equal.
Some prompts outsource effort.
Others strengthen it.

The difference is subtle — but powerful.

A replacement prompt sounds like this:
Write this for me."

A thinking prompt sounds like this:
Help me improve this."
"Point out what I might be missing."
"Challenge this reasoning."
"Organize this so I can see it clearly."
"Ask me questions that would strengthen this idea."

Notice the shift.

In the first, the tool performs.
In the second, the tool supports.

One replaces the process.
The other sharpens it.

Let's make that clearer.

Scenario One: Writing

Before:
Write a proposal for me about expanding our services."

After:
Here is my draft proposal. Help me identify weak sections and suggest ways I can make the argument stronger."

In the first example, the tool creates.
In the second, you lead — the tool refines.

You remain the thinker.
The tool becomes the editor.

Scenario Two: Decision-Making

Before:
What should I do?"
After:
Here are the options I'm considering. Help me think through the pros and cons of each."

In the first example, the tool replaces judgment.
In the second, it organizes your thinking.

The difference is not technical.

It is intentional.

Instead of:
Make the decision."

Try:
Help me think through the options."

Instead of:
Fix this."

Try:
What are three ways this could be clearer?"

Instead of:
Summarize this."

Try:
What are the key arguments, and where might there be gaps?"

These prompts don't eliminate thinking.
They activate it.

They invite structure.
They invite reflection.
They invite refinement.

Scenario Three: Everyday Planning

Before:
Make me a grocery list."

At first, that's exactly what I did.

I would paste the list I had already typed into my phone and say,
Make me a grocery list."

It worked.
But it was basic.

After:
I shop at this store.
Here's what I plan to cook this week.
Organize the list by store sections so I can shop faster, and estimate the total cost so I can stay within my budget."

Nothing about that replaces thinking.

The meals are still mine.
The budget is still mine.
The decisions are still mine.
The tool simply adds structure.

It helps me move more efficiently through a store I already chose,
with a plan I already made.

That's the difference.

Not doing it for you.
Helping you do it better.

The goal is not to become dependent on better prompts.
The goal is to use prompts that make you better.

A thoughtful prompt does not shrink your effort.
It expands your awareness.
It strengthens your judgment.
It sharpens your thinking.

When your thinking sharpens, your work improves.

Not because the tool replaced you.
Because it supported you.
That is the difference.

Chapter 15

The Responsibility of the Thinker

AI can assist you.
It can organize information, challenge assumptions, refine your language, and expand your perspective in ways that would take longer on your own.

But it cannot replace your responsibility.

Thinking is not merely a technical act.
It is a moral one.

When you use a tool, you remain accountable for what you accept, what you repeat, and what you choose to share with others.

Speed does not remove that responsibility.
Convenience does not reduce it.
Capability does not excuse it.

You are still the thinker.

You are still the decision-maker.
You are still the one whose name is attached to the outcome.

AI can support clarity, but clarity is not the same as character.
AI can accelerate output, but acceleration is not the same as wisdom.

Tools amplify what is already present.

If you are careful, it strengthens care.
If you are thoughtful, it sharpens thought.
If you are careless, it accelerates carelessness.

That is not a warning.
It is a reminder.

The future will include more automation, more assistance, and more speed than any previous generation has known.
But no amount of advancement removes the human responsibility to think clearly, verify honestly, and act with integrity.

The strongest users will not be those who memorize the most commands.
They will be those who understand their role.

Not operator — thinker.
Not consumer — leader.
Not replaced — responsible.

The tool can assist.
The responsibility remains yours.

Chapter 16

Use It, Don't Fear It

If you've read this far, you already understand something important.

AI is not magic
It is not a mind.
It is not a moral authority.

It is a tool.

And tools are not meant to be feared.
They are meant to be handled well.

There is a lot of noise surrounding this technology.
Some people treat it like a threat.
Others treat it like a replacement for human effort.

It is neither.

It is assistance.
And assistance does not erase you.

If anything, it reveals you.

When I first began using AI, I didn't fully understand what it was. I assumed it would do more than it should. I also wondered if it might take more than it should.

It didn't.

It reflected what I brought to it.

It responded to my thinking.
It organized what I already carried.
It amplified what I was willing to clarify.

That realization wasn't dramatic.
It was steady.

And it was freeing.

You do not lose yourself when you use this tool.
You lose yourself only when you stop thinking.

And you now know how not to do that.

You know to set boundaries.
You know to verify.
You know to stop.
You know to decide.
You know where your line is.

That is not weakness.
That is leadership.

You do not have to fear something that you understand.

And you do not have to surrender your responsibility to something that cannot carry it for you.

Technology will continue to evolve.
Tools will become faster.
Outputs will become smoother.

But the role of the thinker does not disappear.

You are still the one who decides what to accept.
You are still the one who chooses what to repeat.
You are still the one whose name carries weight.

That has not changed.
It will not change.

So use it.

Use it to clarify your ideas.
Use it to strengthen your preparation.
Use it to challenge your reasoning.
Use it to organize your thinking.

Close it when you need silence.
Pause when you need space.
Step away when the answer is already sufficient.

You are not competing with the tool.
You are guiding it.

You are not behind.
You are not late.
You are not being replaced.

You are learning how to think well in a world with powerful tools.

That is maturity.

And there is something quietly exciting about that.

Because when you use AI thoughtfully, something beautiful happens.
Ideas that felt scattered become structured.
Thoughts that felt trapped become articulated
Questions that felt heavy become organized.

Not because the tool created them.

Because you did.

The tool simply helped you see them more clearly.

You do not have to fear what you can govern.

You do not have to worship what is meant to assist.

You can simply use it well.

Calmly.
Intentionally.
Responsibly.
That is enough.

Made in the USA
Monee, IL
04 November 2026

67386697R00039